Poems
For
Christmas

BY

ELISABETH BURROWES

DORRANCE & COMPANY
Philadelphia

HERE AM I

Here am I, Lord Jesus,
Full of bright dismay
That I have no offering
For Your Christmas Day.

No gem, no golden treasure,
Lamb nor shepherd's crook,
Only these to give You,
My pencil and my book.

CONTENTS

Page

POEMS

FOR CHRISTMAS

ALL OF US

All of us
Hear
The angels
For a little while
At Christmas.

CHRISTMAS
1943

In the deepest of the night
Jesus came;
There was but a little light,
One star-flame.
One star-flame that pointed low
Through the gloom.
Only in the cattle-row
Found he room.

In the silent winter dark,
Angels throng;
All the earth is hushed to mark
Heaven's song,
Heaven's song of Jesus' birth.
He, indeed,
Blesses all the men of earth
At their heed.

Prideful eye and fearful heart
Bid him nay,
From his tender grace depart,
Another way.
Another way—and wandering far
Men despair.
Dies the song, the gleam, the star,
On the air.

Earthward, skyward, spreading wide,
Shadows sweep.
At this holy Christmastide
Darkness deep.
Darkness, deep as folding night
Covers men.
Oh, thou Little Lord of Light,
Come,—again.

CHRISTMAS
1945

So all is done, and in our hearts
The rubble and the pain.
Now, wistful, everyone departs
To Bethlehem again.

There, spent, we kneel before His bed
To find a great release,
To see the glory 'round His head,
The shining of His peace.

Oh, silent wonder of His grace!
Not in the clamorous inn,
But in the low, sweet manger-place
The Lord has ever been.

How gently comes the Christmas morn
As heart to heart, we call,
Rejoice, for Jesus Christ is born,
Whose love shall save us all.

AT THE MANGER

The breath of the beasts was sweet,
And their shaggy coats were warm.
They gave their bodies' heat
For the Babe on Mary's arm.

There by the manger bed
They knelt in the bowery hay.
Kindly they warmed the shed
Where the little Christ-Child lay.

The God of high heaven found fold
Where the least would hardly fare,
And warmth from the winter cold
In the gentle creatures there.

Even I, too, have part
In the wonder of the mow.
Haply my beating heart
Could a little warm Him, now.

NO GAUDY THING

May Christmas be no gaudy thing,
Garish and tinsel-bright,
But decked with love's deep radiance,—
Jesus is born this night.

May it not be a selfish thing,
For me and mine apart,
But given, as Jesus gives it,
To every human heart.

May it not be a moment thing,
Gone with the yule light's blaze,
But a way, a glow, a blessing,
For all our coming days.

RETURN FROM BETHLEHEM

But I wanted power to save me,
That could roar and blind and crush,
Not a star and a midnight hush.

But I wanted a kingly glory,
To fill men's hearts with awe,
Not a babe on a bed of straw.

I wanted a mighty army
With all its strength unfurled,
Not the weakest thing in the world.

HOW ELSEWISE SING?

This is the tend'rest tale
That tongue or book could know.
How elsewise say
Love's advent way?
How elsewise sing
This joyous thing?
Fain so, fain so.

Bright, bright, so bright
That star well might
Pour down for this its light.
Effulgent story
Of angels trailing glory,
Of shepherds running, running
And prophet kings far-riding
To seek this weight of glory.

In this wise shall men see
The Wonder that is He.
To wistful men forlorn
Lo, Christ the Lord is born!
This tender tale most fair,
Immeasured love lies there.
Fain so, fain so,
Ah, it is so, fain so.

VERSE FOR CHRISTMAS

Forever and forever
I was, am, and shall be.

I dwell in light,
Light beyond shadow,
Illimit, pulsing light,
Too all-pervading bright
For those man-eyes
That I so prize.

My clear, transcendent NOW,
Man cannot reason how
It so could be:
Fullness of joy
Beyond his best employ.

For his most human sake
I give what he can take.
My wide eternity
Day-measured thus shall be;
My pure, unshadowed light
Be one small sun,
Soft-curtained in by night;
Joy rimmed by anguish deep,
That he may keep
Heart's tenderness,
His little days to bless;
And, safely set afar,
My Star,
That his stumbling feet be led
To a manger bed.

I go to him
That he may come to me.
So may he, if he will,
My love fulfill.

MAKE ROOM

Make room, ah, room for Christmas.
Clear but a little space,
And light a beaming candle,
And set a rose in place.

So, when the Holy Christ-Child
Comes seeking shelter there
He find a waiting chamber
All garnished for his care,

A still, sweet house of welcome,
A lowly door swung wide,
A place where he may enter
And bring the Christmastide.

(Ancient carol:
"Christmas brings joy to every heart.")

BUT NOT TO MINE

"Christmas brings joy to every heart,"—
But not to mine.
I hold in bitterness apart.
My sorry shrine
Is decked with haste
And anxious thought
And cruel fear.
The Holy Child
Could find Him naught
Of shelter here.

O God, I have not made for Thee
A resting place.
Do Thou, I pray,
Make one for me,
Of Thy great grace.

CHRISTMAS

Comes too early,
Lasts too long.
Hurly-burly
Drowns its song.

Yet it brings us,
Quietly,
Its irradiant
Mystery.

Once again the
Heavenly light:
O Little Town,
And *Silent Night.*

Lift your eyes,
Heart open wide.
Kneel.
Adore.
It is Christmastide.

"Celebrons La Naissance" (Fifteen Century)
Traditional French Carol
(My words, not a translation. E.B.)

O TELL ME NOW GOOD PEOPLE

O tell me now, good people,
What means this burst of song,
And what the heavenly radiance
That streams the hills along?

> The messengers of heaven
> Do say that God is come
> To find on earth His dwelling
> And in our hearts His home.

O tell me, all ye shepherds
Close gathered in affright,
Did you, too, hear the angels,
This strange and holy night?

> Yea, in the glowing heavens
> A wondrous mystery.
> And now we journey straitly
> The promised king to see.

Great sages, westward riding,
What seek you, following far?
O tell us now the meaning
Of that most glowing star.

> The kings of earth are seeking
> A greater one than they,
> Whose kingdom is forever
> And will not pass away.

O tell me, gracious Mary,
What mean these opening skies,
And what the light that shineth
So tender in thine eyes?

     Nay, nay. I cannot tell thee
     What wonder hath been done,
     I only know He sleepeth
     Hereby, my little son.

GENTLE JESUS SLEEPING

Gentle Jesus, sleeping,
Pillowed on the fragrant hay,
Hold us in Thy keeping
As we kneel to pray.

Thou, the Lord of heaven above,
Liest here so weak and small;
From Thy cradle wondrous Love
Shines to save us all.

Gentle Jesus, sleeping,
Pillowed on the fragrant hay,
Hold us in Thy keeping
As we kneel to pray.

(Copyright in *The Pageant Of The Nine Doors.*
Words original, by E.B.)

O LITTLE CRICKET

O little cricket, beneath the doorstone,
Be silent now and cease your cheeping.
The Little Jesus lies in Mary's bosom,
Let all be silent now and make no noise.
He should be sleeping, he should be sleeping,
O little cricket, beneath the doorstone.

(From *The Pageant Of The Nine Doors*,
Mexican traditional.)
Free translation, copyright by E. B.

18

WHERE IS THE ROAD?

Where is the road to Bethlehem?
The little children know.

Wise men wander, traveling far,
Asking, "Why that glowing star?
Does it beckon our questing feet?
Where is the pathway, where the street?"

Sadly the people answer them:
"Where *is* the road to Bethlehem?
We would find it, following, too.
Where, O Wise Men, where go you?"

Seek you the road to Bethlehem?
It is not far to go.
Follow the children, follow them.
The little children know.

WHAT IS CHRISTMAS MADE OF?

Christmas is all gay things—and more:
All that the heart can hold in store;

All that the soul of man can see
Of love and wonder and mystery:

Panoplied riders along the plain,
Camels and kings in a lordly train,

Grazing flocks on the hillside fair,
Shepherds with wondering eyes of prayer,

Angel hosts in the night-blue sky
Singing Glory to God on high,

And a great light shining above the head
Of a Child, low laid in a manger bed.

Sing! For this is the morn of joy!
Christmas is come! Rejoice! Rejoice!

Sing, oh sing, for He brings us joy.
Lift together our heart and voice.

Hand to my hand my brother's hand,
And his to other hand again,

A circling chain through every land.
Thus does the Christ come down to men.

Here to the Christ Child our hearts we lift.
He is the gold, the nard, the gem;

He is the Giver and He the Gift,
He is the Rose of Bethlehem.

Far let the echoes ring and rise,
Farther and farther the chorus swell

Till earth envisions the bending skies.

Oh, come. Oh come, Emanuel.

AS ONCE AGAIN

So it has come and gone, the tender light
That for a moment shone in all our hearts,
Is changing now to common day and night
As once again the Christmastide departs.

Perhaps some day we can at last endure
Continued ecstasy, love's utmost plane,
The height of joy, where joy at last is pure,
And learn from rapture as we did from pain.